Congressional
Research
Service

Tax Provisions to Assist with Disaster Recovery

Erika K. Lunder
Legislative Attorney

Carol A. Pettit
Legislative Attorney

Jennifer Teefy
Information Research Specialist

November 29, 2012

Congressional Research Service

7-5700

www.crs.gov

R42839

Summary

Relief after a natural or man-made disaster may come from what many might consider an unlikely source: the Internal Revenue Code (IRC). The IRC includes several tax relief provisions that apply to affected taxpayers. Some of these provisions are permanent. The following are among the permanent provisions discussed in this report:

- casualty loss deductions, IRC Section 165;

- exemption from taxation for disaster relief payments to individuals, IRC Section 139;

- exemption from taxation for certain insurance payments, IRC Section 123; and

- deferral of gain from the involuntary conversion of homes destroyed or damaged by a disaster, IRC Section 1033.

In recent years, Congress has enacted tax legislation generally intended to assist victims of specific disasters; as a result, these laws were temporary in nature. One act, however, provided more general, but still temporary, relief for any federally declared disaster occurring prior to January 1, 2010. The acts providing temporary relief include the following:

- The Job Creation and Worker Assistance Act of 2002, P.L. 107-147, which provided tax benefits for areas of New York City damaged by the terrorist attacks of September 11, 2001;

- The Katrina Emergency Tax Relief Act of 2005 (KETRA), P.L. 109-73, which provided tax relief to assist the victims of Hurricane Katrina in 2005;

- The Gulf Opportunity Zone (GO Zone) Act of 2005, P.L. 109-135, which provided tax relief to those affected by Hurricanes Katrina, Rita, and Wilma in 2005; and

- The Heartland Disaster Tax Relief Act of 2008, P.L. 110-343, which provided tax relief to assist recovery from both the severe weather that affected the Midwest during the summer of 2008 and Hurricane Ike. This act also included general disaster tax relief provisions that applied to federally declared disasters occurring before January 1, 2010.

This report provides a basic overview of existing, permanent provisions that benefit victims of disasters, as well as past, targeted legislative responses to particular disasters. The relief is discussed without examining either the qualifications for or the limitation on claiming the provisions' benefits. In light of Hurricane Sandy, this report is designed to help Congress identify previous legislative responses to recent disasters.

Contents

Tables

Appendixes

Contacts

The Internal Revenue Code (IRC) includes several permanent provisions that become relevant when taxpayers are affected by disasters. For example, individuals are generally not taxed on disaster relief payments, and taxpayers whose homes are destroyed by disasters may be able to defer any gain arising from an involuntary conversion.

In recent years, Congress has enacted temporary tax legislation intended to assist victims of disasters. Most often, these temporary provisions applied to specific, identified disasters (e.g., Hurricane Katrina). However, in 2008, as part of legislation targeting specific disasters, Congress also enacted temporary provisions that applied generally to federally declared disasters occurring prior to January 1, 2010.[1] The following is a list of the primary laws that have provided relief:

- The Job Creation and Worker Assistance Act of 2002 (Job Creation Act), P.L. 107-147, which provided tax benefits for areas of New York City damaged by the terrorist attacks of September 11, 2001;

- The Katrina Emergency Tax Relief Act of 2005 (KETRA), P.L. 109-73, which provided tax relief intended to assist businesses and individuals affected by Hurricane Katrina in 2005 and permanently extended the authority of the Internal Revenue Service (IRS) to postpone certain deadlines;

- The Gulf Opportunity Zone Act of 2005 (GO Zone Act), P.L. 109-135, which provided tax relief intended to assist businesses and individuals affected by Hurricanes Katrina, Rita, and Wilma in 2005; and

- The Heartland Disaster Tax Relief Act of 2008 and other provisions in P.L. 110-343 (Heartland Act), which provided tax relief intended to assist with the recovery from the severe weather that affected the Midwest during the summer of 2008 and Hurricane Ike,[2] as well as including some general disaster tax relief provisions for federally declared disasters occurring prior to January 1, 2010.[3]

This report is intended to assist Congress by identifying provisions that have been enacted to respond to past disasters. As such, it provides only a basic overview of the permanent and temporary provisions. It does not discuss the provisions' qualifications, limitations, and deadlines. For example, some of the laws distinguished between the areas the President determined warranted only public assistance under the Stafford Act, and those areas determined to warrant individual or individual and public assistance, with the latter areas eligible for additional benefits, and these types of distinctions are not noted in the report.[4] The report makes no attempt to evaluate the wisdom, efficacy, or fairness of any of the provisions.

The report is divided into three sections: (1) selected permanent disaster tax provisions; (2) temporary provisions that applied generally to disasters; and (3) temporary provisions targeting specific disasters. The **Appendix** contains a table that indicates which temporary provisions were included in each act.

---

[1].P.L. 110-343, Div. C ("Tax Extenders and Alternative Minimum Tax Relief Act of 2008"), Title VII, Subtitle B

[2] P.L. 110-343, Div. C ("Tax Extenders and Alternative Minimum Tax Relief Act of 2008"), Title VII, Subtitle A. The act also imposed a permanent requirement that §501(c)(3) charitable organizations report information on their disaster relief activities and contributions on the annual information return (Form 990) filed with the IRS. *See id* at §703 (codified at 26 U.S.C. §6033(b)(14)).

[3] P.L. 110-343, Div. C ("Tax Extenders and Alternative Minimum Tax Relief Act of 2008"), Title VII, Subtitle B.

[4] *See, e.g.,* P.L. 110-343, Div. C, Title VII, Subtitle A, §702(b).

Permanent Provisions

Disaster Assistance Payments to Individuals

Section 139 of the IRC exempts qualified disaster relief payments from the recipient's income. These include payments made to, or for the benefit of, an individual (1) to reimburse or pay for reasonable and necessary personal, family, living, or funeral expenses incurred as a result of a qualified disaster; (2) to reimburse or pay for reasonable and necessary expenses incurred for the repair or rehabilitation of a personal residence or repair or replacement of its contents to the extent that the need for such repair, rehabilitation, or replacement is attributable to a qualified disaster; and (3) by a federal, state, or local government in connection with a qualified disaster in order to promote the general welfare. The exclusion applies only to expenses not compensated for by insurance or otherwise.

A qualified disaster is one determined by the President to warrant federal assistance under the Stafford Act and, for the third type of payment, a disaster determined by an appropriate federal, state, or local authority to warrant government assistance.

Certain Insurance Payments

For a taxpayer whose principal residence is damaged or destroyed by storm or other casualty, or who is denied access to the residence by governmental authorities because of the occurrence or threat of occurrence of such a casualty, gross income does not include payments made under an insurance contract to compensate or reimburse the individual for household living expenses resulting from the loss of use or occupancy of the residence.[5] This exclusion applies only to the extent the amount received does not exceed the amount by which the actual living expenses incurred during the period of non-use or occupancy exceed the normal living expenses that would have been incurred. In other words, the excluded amount generally represents expenses actually incurred due to the casualty for renting housing and paying extraordinary expenses for such things as food and transportation.

Casualty Loss, Involuntary Conversion, Etc.

Several provisions may apply in disaster situations, such as the provisions that permit taxpayers to deduct casualty losses and defer gain on involuntary conversions. Although the general provisions are permanent,[6] Congress has enacted special temporary rules regarding aspects of these provisions in the Job Creation Act, KETRA, the GO Zone Act, and the Heartland Act. For this reason, these provisions are discussed below (see "Casualty Losses," "Involuntary Conversions").

---

[5] 26 U.S.C. §123; 26 C.F.R. §1.123-1.

[6] *See, e.g.,* 26 U.S.C. §§165 (casualty losses), 1033 (involuntary conversions).

IRS Authority to Suspend Deadlines

The Internal Revenue Service (IRS) has the express statutory authority to postpone tax-related deadlines for certain taxpayers, including those affected by a federally declared disaster.[7] These deadlines include those for filing returns and making payments for income, gift, and estate taxes. Prior to KETRA, income taxes withheld at source and employment taxes were explicitly excluded from this authority, and excise taxes were not mentioned. KETRA permanently granted the IRS the authority to postpone deadlines related to these taxes.[8]

Underpayment of Income Tax

An individual who underpays his or her estimated income tax is subject to a penalty equal to the interest that would accrue on the underpayment, for the period of the underpayment.[9] The IRS is authorized to waive the underpayment penalty for underpayments due to casualty, disaster, or other unusual circumstance if the imposition of the penalty would be inequitable and against good conscience.[10]

Retirement Plan Rollovers

Rollover distributions from tax-deferred retirement plans and individual retirement accounts must generally be transferred to an eligible plan within 60 days to avoid incurring income tax and penalties.[11] However, the Secretary of the Treasury (Secretary) has the statutory authority to waive the 60-day period in hardship situations where failure to waive the deadline would be against equity or good conscience.[12] Events that could be considered hardships include casualties, disasters, and other events beyond the reasonable control of the individual subject to the rollover deadline.

General Provisions That Have Recently Expired

Provisions Applicable to Federally Declared Disasters Occurring Prior to January 1, 2010

The Heartland Act contained several provisions that generally applied to federally declared disasters declared after December 31, 2007, and before January 1, 2010.[13] These provisions

---

[7] 26 U.S.C. §§7508, 7508A.

[8] KETRA, P.L. 109-73, Title IV, §403. Additionally, KETRA and the GO Zone act mandated that the IRS use this authority to extend deadlines to February 28, 2006. KETRA, P.L. 109-73, Title IV, §403; GO Zone, P.L. 109-135, Title II, §201(a) (codified at 26 U.S.C. §1400S(c)).

[9] 26 U.S.C. §6654.

[10] 26 U.S.C. §6654(e)(3)(A).

[11] 26 U.S.C. §§402, 408.

[12] 26 U.S.C. §§402(c)(3)(B), 408(d)(3)(I).

[13] Some, but not all, of these provisions applied to the 2008 Midwest storms and Hurricane Ike. P.L. 110-343, Div. C ("Tax Extenders and Alternative Minimum Tax Relief Act of 2008"), Title VII, Subtitle B, §712. As discussed in this (continued...)

---

created temporary rules for casualty losses, expensing, net operating losses, bonus depreciation, and mortgage revenue bonds.

Additionally, the Heartland Act, KETRA, and the GO Zone Act sometimes created special rules for these same provisions applicable to the specific disasters covered by those acts. These are mentioned in the footnotes.

Casualty Losses

Taxpayers may deduct unreimbursed losses of property not connected to a trade or business when the losses are from a casualty, such as a hurricane.[14] In addition to losses from the actual damage caused by the casualty, an individual may have a casualty loss if ordered by the state to demolish or relocate the home and such order comes within 120 days of the federal declaration that the location is a disaster area.

To determine the amount of the loss, two values are compared: decrease in fair market value (FMV) as a result of the casualty and the taxpayer's adjusted basis in the property (i.e., the cost of the property with certain adjustments).[15] The lower amount is the amount of the loss, subject to several limitations: (1) the first $100 of each loss is not deductible and (2) only the aggregate amount of the net loss (after applying the $100 limitation and offsetting casualty gains) that exceeds 10% of adjusted gross income is deductible.

The deduction is generally claimed in the year of the loss. However, a loss in a federally declared disaster area may be deducted in the year prior to the disaster.[16]

The Heartland Act made three changes for individuals affected by federally declared disasters occurring prior to January 1, 2010: (1) it waived the 10% restriction; (2) it increased the standard deduction by the amount of such losses (thus permitting individuals who did not itemize deductions to deduct their losses); and (3) it increased the $100 floor to $500.[17]

Expensing

In general, capital expenditures must be added to a property's basis rather than being expensed (i.e., deducted in the current year). IRC Section 179 provides an exception so that a business may expense the costs of certain property in the year it is placed in service. In general, the total cost of the Section 179 property cannot exceed $125,000, and the deduction is decreased by one dollar for every dollar that the total cost of all property the business placed in service during the year exceeds $500,000—both numbers are adjusted for inflation. The Heartland Act increased the

---

(...continued)

report, the Heartland Act also provided special rules for these two disasters.

[14] 26 U.S.C. §165.

[15] For a discussion of basis, see CRS Report RL34662, *Tax Basis: What Is It? Why Is It Important?*, by Carol A. Pettit.

[16] 26 U.S.C. §165(e).

[17] Heartland Act, P.L. 110-343, Div. C, Title VII, Subtitle B, §706. Meanwhile, KETRA and the GO Zone Act had waived the $100 and 10% floors for casualty losses from the 2005 hurricanes. KETRA, P.L. 109-73, Title IV, §402; GO Zone Act, P.L. 109-135, Title II, §201(a) (codified at 26 U.S.C. §1400S(b)). The Heartland Act had similarly waived the $100 limitation for the 2008 Midwest storms. Heartland Act, P.L. 110-343, Div. C, Title VII, Subtitle B, §711.

Section 179 limitations by up to $100,000 and $600,000 for qualified disaster area property for federally declared disasters occurring prior to January 1, 2010.[18]

The Heartland Act also added IRC Section 198A, which permits full expensing (subject to depreciation recapture) of qualified expenditures for the abatement or control of hazardous substances released on account of a federally declared disaster, the removal of debris or the demolition of structures on business-related real property damaged by such a disaster, and the repair of business-related property damaged by such a disaster.[19] This provision only applied to federally declared disasters occurring prior to January 1, 2010.

Net Operating Losses

In general, a taxpayer's net operating loss (NOL) may be carried back and deducted in the two tax years before the NOL year, and then carried forward for up to 20 years after the NOL year.[20] These methods are known as "carrybacks" and "carryovers," respectively.

The carryback period is extended to three years for individuals who have a loss of property arising from a casualty or theft.[21] A three-year period also applies for small businesses and farmers for NOLs attributable to federally declared disasters.[22]

The Heartland Act provided for a five-year carryback period for qualified losses from any federally declared disaster occurring prior to January 1, 2010.[23] For such disasters, it also suspended the alternative minimum tax (AMT) provision that generally limits NOL deductions to 90% of alternative minimum taxable income.[24]

Bonus Depreciation

Taxpayers who acquire certain types of property may claim an additional depreciation amount equal to 50% of the property's adjusted basis for the year the property is placed in service.[25] This

---

[18] Heartland Act, P.L. 110-343, Div. C, Title VII, Subtitle B, §711. The GO Zone did the same for GO Zone property, while Job Creation Act increased the limitations by lesser amounts for New York Liberty Zone property. GO Zone Act, P.L. 109-135, Title I, §101(a) (codified at 26 U.S.C. §1400N(e)); Job Creation Act, P.L. 107-147, Title III, §301(a) (codified at 26 U.S.C. §1400L(f)).

[19] Heartland Act, P.L. 110-343, Div. C, Title VII, Subtitle B, §707. Meanwhile, both the GO Zone Act and the Heartland Act allowed taxpayers to expense 50% of qualified clean-up costs for the removal of debris or the demolition of structures on business real property in the applicable hurricane or Midwestern disaster zones. GO Zone Act, P.L. 109-135, Title I, §101(a) (codified at 26 U.S.C. §1400N(f)); Heartland Act, P.L. 110-343, Div. C, Title VII, Subtitle A, §702(d)(3), (4).

[20] 26 U.S.C. §172.

[21] 26 U.S.C. §172(b)(1)(F).

[22] *See id.*

[23] Heartland Act, P.L. 110-343, Div. C, Title VII, Subtitle B, §708 (codified at 26 U.S.C. §172(b)(1)(J)). The act also provided similar rules for qualified Midwest disaster losses. Heartland Act, P.L. 110-343, Div. C, Title VII, Subtitle A, §702(d)(6). The GO Zone Act had allowed NOLs from the hurricanes to be carried back for five years. GO Zone Act, P.L. 109-135, Title I, §101(a) (codified at 26 U.S.C. §1400N(k)).

[24] 26 U.S.C. §56(d); Heartland Act, P.L. 110-343, Div. C, Title VII, Subtitle B, §708 (codified at 26 U.S.C. §56(d)(3).

[25] 26 U.S.C. §168(k). For information on bonus depreciation, see CRS Report RL31852, *Section 179 and Bonus Depreciation Expensing Allowances: Current Law, Legislative Proposals in the 112th Congress, and Economic Effects*, by Gary Guenther.

---

is commonly referred to as "bonus depreciation." The Heartland Act provided a 50% bonus depreciation provision for qualified property from a federally declared disaster occurring prior to January 1, 2010.[26]

Mortgage Revenue Bonds

Mortgage revenue bonds are tax-exempt bonds used to finance below-market rate mortgages for low and moderate-income homebuyers.[27] In general, the homebuyers must not have owned a residence for the past three years, and the houses' costs may not exceed 90% of the average purchase price for the area. However, for areas that are low-income or of chronic economic distress, the three-year restriction does not apply and the purchase price limitation is increased to 110%.[28]

For individuals whose homes were declared unsafe or ordered to be demolished or relocated due to a federally declared disaster occurring prior to January 1, 2010, the Heartland Act waived the three-year restriction and increased the purchase price limitation from 90% to 110%.[29] It also permitted individuals whose homes were damaged by the disaster to treat the amount of owner-financing provided for home repair and construction as a qualified rehabilitation loan, limited to $150,000 (the amount is generally limited to $15,000),[30] which had the effect of waiving the three-year requirement for such financing.

Other Recently Expired General Provisions

In addition to the Heartland Act's provisions that generally applied to any federally declared disaster declared after December 31, 2007, and before January 1, 2010, other provisions in federal law have provided temporary relief that were generally available (i.e., not restricted to specific disasters).

Expensing of Environmental Remediation Costs

As mentioned above, capital expenditures must generally be added to the property's basis rather than being expensed (i.e., deducted in the current year). IRC Section 198 provided another exception by allowing taxpayers to expense any qualifying environmental remediation costs paid or incurred prior to January 1, 2012, for the abatement or control of hazardous substances at a qualified contaminated site. Unlike the other expensing provisions discussed above (Sections 179

---

[26] Heartland Act, P.L. 110-343, Div. C, Title VII, Subtitle B, §710 (codified at 26 U.S.C. §168(n)). The GO Zone Act also provided a 50% bonus depreciation provision for qualified property, as well as granting the Secretary the authority to suspend the deadline by which property must be placed in service, on a case-by-case basis, for up to one year for taxpayers affected by the hurricanes. GO Zone Act, P.L. 109-135, Title I, §101(a) (codified at 26 U.S.C. §1400N(d)). The Job Creation Act had provided for 30% additional depreciation. Job Creation Act, P.L. 107-147, Title III, §301(a) (codified at 26 U.S.C. §1400L(b)).

[27] 26 U.S.C. §143.

[28] 26 U.S.C. §143(d)(2)(A), (e)(5).

[29] P.L. 110-343, §709. KETRA and the GO Zone Act temporarily removed the three-year requirement for qualifying homes, as well as increasing the limitation on qualified home improvement loans from $15,000 to $150,000 for loans used to repair hurricane damage. KETRA, P.L. 109-73, Title IV, §404; GO Zone Act, P.L. 109-135, Title I, §104.

[30] 26 U.S.C. §143(d)(2)(B).

---

and 198A), Section 198 is not limited to federally declared disasters or specific disasters. The provision was enacted as a temporary one and has been extended several times, but has now expired.

The Heartland Act was among those laws that temporarily extended Section 198.[31] The GO Zone Act had also extended the provision, but only for those costs for contaminated sites in the GO Zone, as well as treating petroleum products as a hazardous substance.[32]

Charitable Contributions of Inventory

In general, donors of food inventory who are not C corporations may only claim a charitable deduction that equals their basis in the inventory (typically, its cost).[33] C corporations may deduct the lesser of (1) the basis plus 50% of the property's appreciated value or (2) two times basis.

KETRA provided special rules that allowed donors of wholesome food inventory to benefit from this enhanced deduction and allowed C corporations to claim an enhanced deduction for donations of book inventory to public schools.[34] Neither provision was limited to donations related to the hurricane, but both were originally set to expire on December 31, 2005. The provisions have been extended several times since then, including by the Heartland Act (as part of its tax extenders package, rather than its disaster relief provisions).[35] Most recently, both provisions were extended through December 31, 2011.[36]

Provisions Targeting Specific Disasters

Involuntary Conversions

An involuntary conversion occurs when property is converted to money or other property because of its complete or partial destruction, theft, seizure, or condemnation, or if it is disposed of under threat of condemnation.[37] An example of an involuntary conversion is when an individual receives an insurance payment for damaged property. If the cash or property that was received is worth less than the basis of the property that was converted, the taxpayer has a loss, which may qualify for deduction under the casualty loss rules discussed above. If the cash or property received is worth more than the basis of the property that was converted, then the taxpayer has realized a gain, which may or may not be immediately includable in gross income ("recognized").

---

[31] Heartland Act, P.L. 110-343, Div. C, Title III, §318.

[32] GO Zone Act, P.L. 109-135, Title I, §101(a) (codified at 26 U.S.C. §1400N(g)).

[33] IRC §170(e). For more information on the charitable contribution deduction, see CRS Report RL34608, *Tax Issues Relating to Charitable Contributions and Organizations*, by Jane G. Gravelle and Molly F. Sherlock.

[34] KETRA, P.L. 109-73, Title III, §§305 (codified at 26 U.S.C. §170 (e)(3)(C)(iv)), 306 (codified at 26 U.S.C. §170(e)(3)(D)(iv)).

[35] Heartland Act, P.L. 110-343, Div. C, Title III, §§323, 324.

[36] P.L. 111-312 ("Tax Relief, Unemployment Insurance Reauthorization, and Job Creation Act of 2010"), Subtitle C, §§740(a), 741(a).

[37] 26 U.S.C. §1033.

There are no immediate tax consequences if the property is converted to property that is similar or related in service or use ("similar property").[38] If, on the other hand, the property is involuntarily converted to cash or dissimilar property, the taxpayer must recognize any gain unless purchasing similar property within a certain time period. If the taxpayer purchases the replacement property in a timely manner, an election is available that allows recognition of gain only to the extent that the amount realized from the involuntary conversion exceeds the cost of the new property. The time period is generally two years.

Taxpayers whose principal residence or any of its contents are involuntarily converted as a result of a federally declared disaster qualify for three special rules.[39] First, gain realized from the receipt of insurance proceeds for unscheduled personal property (property in the home that is not listed as being covered under the insurance policy) is not recognized. Second, any other insurance proceeds received for the residence or its contents are treated as a common fund. If the fund is used to purchase property that is similar or related in service or use to the converted residence or its contents, then the owner may elect to recognize gain only to the extent that the common fund exceeds the cost of the replacement property. Third, the replacement period for property involuntarily converted as a result of a federally declared disaster is four years rather than two.

If a taxpayer's business property is involuntarily converted as a result of a federally declared disaster, then the taxpayer is not required to replace it with property that is similar or related in service to the original property in order to avoid having to recognize gain on the conversion, as long as the replacement property is still held for a type of business purpose.[40] The replacement period for business property is two years after the close of the first tax year in which any part of the conversion gain is realized (the replacement period for *condemned* business property is three years).

The Job Creation Act, KETRA, and the Heartland Act increased the two-year time period to purchase the replacement property to five years for property in the applicable disaster area so long as substantially all of the use of the replacement property occurs in such area.[41]

Discharge of Indebtedness

When all or part of a debt is forgiven, the amount of the cancellation is ordinarily included in the income of the taxpayer receiving the benefit of the discharge.[42] However, there are several exceptions to this general rule. For example, no amount of the discharge is included in income if the cancellation is intended to be a gift or is from the discharge of student loans for the

---

[38] The taxpayer's basis in the new property is the same as in the converted property; thus, he or she is able to defer recognition of any gain until he or she sells or exchanges the new property.

[39] 26 U.S.C. §1033(h). Additionally, under 26 U.S.C. §121, individuals may exclude up to $250,000 ($500,000 if married filing jointly) of gain from selling a principal residence if the taxpayer meets a use test (has lived in the house for at least two years out of the last five years) and an ownership test (has owned the house, also for two years out of the last five). If a taxpayer fails to meet the use test but experiences an unforeseen circumstance, the taxpayer may claim a reduced exclusion. Unforeseen circumstances include the involuntary conversion of a residence and a natural or man-made disaster (or act of war or terrorism) resulting in a casualty to a principal residence. *See* 26 C.F.R. §1.121-3(e)(2).

[40] 26 U.S.C. §1033(h).

[41] Job Creation Act, P.L. 107-147, Title III, §301(a) (codified at 26 U.S.C. §1400L(g)); KETRA, P.L. 109-73, Title IV, §405; Heartland Act, P.L. 110-343, Div. C, Title VII, Subtitle A, §702(e)(5).

[42] 26 U.S.C. §61(a)(12).

---

performance of qualifying services.[43] There are also certain situations in which the taxpayer may defer taxation, with the possibility of permanent exclusion, on income from the discharge of indebtedness, such as if discharge occurs when the debtor is in Title 11 bankruptcy proceedings or legally insolvent.[44] Both KETRA and the Heartland Act included provisions that allowed victims to exclude non-business debt forgiveness from income in certain conditions.

Victims of Hurricane Katrina were allowed to exclude non-business debt that was forgiven by a governmental agency or certain financial institutions if the discharge occurred after August 24, 2005, and before January 1, 2007.[45] Individuals were eligible for this benefit if (1) their principal place of abode was in the core disaster area or (2) it was in the Hurricane Katrina disaster area and they suffered an economic loss due to the hurricane. Individuals with certain tax attributes (such as basis) were required to reduce them by the amount excluded from income, which has the effect of deferring (rather than permanently eliminating) the tax on the cancelled debt.

For victims with a principal place of abode in a Midwestern disaster area, the Heartland Act provided similar relief. However, if that home was in an area determined by the President to warrant only public assistance, the individual also had to have suffered an economic loss due to the severe weather.[46]

Retirement Plan Distributions

KETRA, the GO Zone Act, and the Heartland Act all provided relief relating to retirement plan distributions. First, each act waived the 10% penalty that would otherwise apply on early withdrawals made from a qualifying retirement plan[47] if the individual's principal place of abode was in the disaster area and the individual sustained an economic loss due to the disaster.[48] The distributions were required to occur within a specified time frame, and the maximum amount that could be withdrawn without penalty was $100,000. Funds could be re-contributed to a qualified plan over a three-year period and receive tax-free rollover treatment. Additionally, with respect to any taxable portion of the distribution, the individual could include one-third of such amount in gross income over the course of three tax years rather than including the entire amount on the tax return for the year of distribution.

Additionally, the acts permitted individuals who had received qualifying distributions to buy or construct a principal residence in the applicable disaster area, but were prevented from doing so by the disaster, to re-contribute the funds to a qualified plan without tax consequences.[49]

Further, the acts increased the amount disaster victims could borrow from their retirement plans without immediate tax consequences.[50] Under current law, the maximum amount that may be

---

[43] 26 U.S.C. §§102, 108.

[44] 26 U.S.C. §108(a).

[45] KETRA, P.L. 109-73, Title IV, §401.

[46] Heartland Act, P.L. 110-343, Div. C, Title VII, Subtitle A, §702(e)(4).

[47] 26 U.S.C. §72(t).

[48] KETRA, P.L. 109-73, Title I, §101; GO Zone Act, P.L. 109-135, Title II, §201(a) (codified at 26 U.S.C. §1400Q(a)); Heartland Act, P.L. 110-343, Div. C, Title VII, Subtitle A, §702(d)(10).

[49] KETRA, P.L. 109-73, Title I, §102; GO Zone Act, P.L. 109-135, Title II, §201(a) (codified at 26 U.S.C. §1400Q(b)); Heartland Act, P.L. 110-343, Div. C, Title VII, Subtitle A, §702(d)(10).

[50] 26 U.S.C. §72(p).

borrowed without being treated as a taxable distribution is the lesser of (a) $50,000, reduced by certain outstanding loans or (b) the greater of $10,000 or 50% of the present value of the employee's nonforfeitable accrued benefits. For loans made during the applicable period, the acts increased this to the lesser of (1) $100,000, reduced by certain outstanding loans, or (2) the greater of $10,000 or 100% of the present value of the employee's nonforfeitable accrued benefits, as well as extending certain loan repayment dates by one year.[51]

Employment Relief

Work Opportunity Tax Credit

Generally, businesses that hire individuals from groups with high unemployment rates or special employment needs, such as high-risk youths and veterans, may claim the work opportunity tax credit.[52] The credit may be claimed for the wages of up to $6,000 that were paid during the employee's first year. For an employee who worked at least 400 hours, the credit equals 40% of his or her wages—thus, the maximum credit is $2,400. For an employee who worked from 120 to 399 hours, the credit equals 25% of his or her wages. The credit does not apply to wages paid after December 31, 2012.

KETRA allowed businesses to claim the work opportunity credit on wages paid to certain employees hired after Hurricane Katrina.[53] Eligible employees were those who had a principal place of abode in the core disaster area and either (1) were hired during the two-year period beginning August 28, 2005, for a position in the area or (2) were displaced by the Hurricane and are hired after August 27, 2005, and before January 1, 2006. The Job Creation Act provided similar treatment for New York Liberty Zone business employees and certain employees outside the zone.[54]

Retention Credit

KETRA, the GO Zone Act, and the Heartland Act all provided a temporary retention credit for disaster-damaged businesses that continued to pay wages to their employees who were unable to continue in their jobs after the storm had rendered the business currently inoperable.[55] Eligible employees were those whose principal place of employment was in the applicable disaster area. The credit equaled 40% of the employee's first $6,000 in wages paid between the date the business became inoperable and the date it resumed significant operations at that location (or the end of the first calendar year, whichever came first). The credits were generally limited to those employers who employed no more than 200 employees per day during the year before the disaster.

---

[51] KETRA, P.L. 109-73, Title I, §103; GO Zone Act, P.L. 109-135, §201(a) (codified at 26 U.S.C. §1400Q(c)); Heartland Act, P.L. 110-343, Div. C, Title VII, Subtitle A, §702(d)(10).

[52] 26 U.S.C. §51. For more information, see CRS Report RL30089, *The Work Opportunity Tax Credit (WOTC)*, by Christine Scott.

[53] KETRA, P.L. 109-73, Title II, §201.

[54] Job Creation Act, P.L. 107-147, Title III, §301(a) (codified at 26 U.S.C. §1400L(a)).

[55] KETRA, P.L. 109-73, Title II, §202; GO Zone Act, P.L. 109-135, Title II, §201(a) (codified at 26 U.S.C. §1400R); Heartland Act, P.L. 110-343, Div. C, Title VII, Subtitle A, §702(d)(11).

Employer-Provided Housing

Both the GO Zone Act and the Heartland Act excluded the value of certain employer-provided housing, limited to $600 per month, from the employee's income and allowed the employer to claim a credit equal to 30% of that amount.[56] Among other requirements, the employee must have had a principal residence in the applicable disaster area and have performed substantially all employment services for that employer in that area. The employer must have had a trade or business located within the applicable disaster area.

Bonds

Tax-Exempt Bonds

Both the GO Zone Act and the Heartland Act temporarily allowed affected states to issue tax-exempt bonds to finance (1) qualified activities involving residential rental projects, nonresidential real property, and public utility property located in the disaster area and (2) below-market rate mortgages for low- and moderate-income homebuyers.[57] Under the GO Zone Act, the maximum amount of bonds that each state could issue was $2,500 multiplied by that state's population that was located in the GO Zone as determined prior to the date of Hurricane Katrina. Under the Heartland Act, the maximum amount of bonds each state could issue was capped at $1,000 multiplied by that state's population in the disaster area, and the act expressly stated that the bonds would have to be designated by the appropriate state authority on the basis of providing assistance to where it was most needed. The Job Creation Act, meanwhile, allowed New York to issue up to $8 billion (divided equally between the state and New York City) in tax-exempt bonds to finance qualified activities involving residential rental projects, nonresidential real property, and public utility property located in the disaster zone.[58] The Job Creation Act and the GO Zone Act also allowed one additional advance refunding of qualifying bonds that were issued by those states and were outstanding on the date of Hurricane Katrina.[59]

The GO Zone Act and the Heartland Act allowed operators of low-income residential rental projects financed by IRC Section 142(d) bonds to rely on the representations of displaced individuals regarding their income qualifications so long as the tenancy began within six months of the displacement.[60]

---

[56] GO Zone Act, P.L. 109-135, Title I, §103 (codified at 26 U.S.C. §1400P).

[57] GO Zone Act, P.L. 109-135, Title I, §101(a) (codified at 26 U.S.C. §1400N(a)); Heartland Act, P.L. 110-343, Div. C, Title VII, Subtitle A, §702(a)(1). The Heartland Act also allowed states affected by Hurricane Ike (Texas and Louisiana) to issue bonds, capped at $2,000 multiplied by the portion of the state's population in specified counties. P.L. 110-343, Div. C, Title VII, Subtitle A, §704.

[58] Job Creation Act, P.L. 107-147, Title III, §301(a) (codified at 26 U.S.C. §1400L(d)).

[59] Job Creation Act, P.L. 107-147, Title III, §301(a) (codified at 26 U.S.C. §1400L(e)); GO Zone Act, P.L. 109-135, Title I, §101(a) (codified at 26 U.S.C. §1400N(b)).

[60] GO Zone Act, P.L. 109-135, Title I, §101(a) (codified at 26 U.S.C. §1400N(n)); Heartland Act, P.L. 110-343, Div. C, Title VII, Subtitle A, §702(a)(1).

Tax Credit Bonds

Both the GO Zone Act and the Heartland Act permitted affected states to issue tax credit bonds to pay the principal, interest, or premiums on qualified governmental bonds or to make loans to political subdivisions to make such payments.[61] Bondholders may claim a credit based on the product of a credit rate and the bonds' outstanding face amount. The bonds were required to be issued within a certain time period and could not have a maturity date beyond two years, among other requirements. Further, each state was capped in the amount of bonds it could be issued—for example, under the Heartland Act, the maximum amount of bonds that could be issued by states with disaster area populations of at least 2 million was $100 million; the cap was $50 million for states with disaster area populations between 1 million and 2 million; and the other states could not issue any bonds. Bonds could not be used for certain activities (e.g., golf courses).

Gulf Coast Recovery Bonds

The GO Zone stated that it was the sense of Congress that the Treasury Secretary designate at least one series of bonds as Gulf Coast Recovery Bonds.[62]

Charitable Giving Incentives

Limits on Charitable Deductions

Taxpayers are generally permitted to deduct contributions made to 501(c)(3) charitable organizations, subject to various limitations.[63] Individuals may not claim a charitable deduction that exceeds 50% of their "contribution base" (adjusted gross income with certain adjustments) and corporations may not claim a deduction that exceeds 10% of their taxable income with certain adjustments. Any excess contributions may generally be carried forward for five years.

KETRA and the GO Zone Act temporarily suspended the 50% and 10% limitations for cash contributions.[64] For individuals, the deduction could not exceed the amount that the contribution base exceeded other charitable contributions. For corporations, the deduction was only allowed for contributions used for hurricane relief efforts and could not exceed the amount that taxable income exceeded other contributions. The acts also suspended the overall limitation on itemized deductions. The Heartland Act provided similar rules for donations for Midwest disaster relief.[65]

---

[61] GO Zone Act, P.L. 109-135, Title I, §101(a) (codified at 26 U.S.C. §1400N(l)); Heartland Act, P.L. 110-343, Div. C, Title VII, Subtitle A, §702(d)(7). For information on tax credit bonds, see CRS Report R40523, *Tax Credit Bonds: Overview and Analysis*, by Steven Maguire.

[62] GO Zone Act, P.L. 109-135, Title III, §301.

[63] 26 U.S.C. §170.

[64] KETRA, P.L. 109-73, Title III, §301; GO Zone Act, P.L. 109-135, Title II, §201(a) (at 26 U.S.C. §1400S(a)).

[65] Heartland Act, P.L. 110-343, Div. C, Title VII, Subtitle A, §702(d)(12).

Housing Exemption

Both KETRA[66] and the Heartland Act[67] provided tax relief to those who provided free housing to those who had been displaced by the storms. Individuals could claim additional personal exemptions of $500 each for up to four displaced people who they housed for at least 60 consecutive days. These exemptions could be claimed in both the year of the disaster and the next year; however, no person could qualify the taxpayer for the exemption in both years. Among other requirements, the displaced person must have had a principal place of abode in the disaster area; if the home was not in the *core* disaster area, then the person must have been displaced due to either storm damage to the home or evacuation caused by the storm.

Mileage Rate and Reimbursement

Generally, individuals who use their personal vehicles for charitable purposes may claim a deduction based on the number of miles driven. The amount is set by statute at 14 cents per mile.[68]

KETRA and the Heartland Act each temporarily increase the charitable mileage rate to 70% of the standard business mileage rate if the vehicle was used for hurricane or Midwest disaster relief.[69] The standard business mileage rate is periodically set by the IRS and is 55.5 cents per mile for 2012[70] and 56.5 cents per mile for 2013.[71]

Additionally, both acts provided a temporary exclusion from a charitable volunteer's gross income for any qualifying mileage reimbursements received from the charity for the operating expenses of the volunteer's passenger automobile for such disaster relief.[72]

Leasehold Improvements

For purposes of depreciation, the Job Creation Act generally shortened the recovery period for leasehold improvement property to five years for qualifying property located in the New York disaster zone.[73]

Credit Computations

KETRA, the GO Zone Act, and the Heartland Act permitted qualifying disaster victims to elect to use their earned income from the year prior to the disaster for computing the child tax credit and

---

[66] KETRA, P.L. 109-73, Title III, §302.

[67] Heartland Act, P.L. 110-343, Div. C, Title VII, Subtitle A, §702(a)(2) (extending certain benefits included in KETRA to the Midwestern disaster area).

[68] 26 U.S.C. §170(i).

[69] KETRA, P.L. 109-73, Title III, §303; Heartland Act, P.L. 110-343, Div. C, Title VII, Subtitle A, §702(e)(2).

[70] IRS News Release IR 2011-116 (Dec. 9, 2011).

[71] IRS News Release IR 2012-95 (Nov. 21, 2012).

[72] KETRA, P.L. 109-73, Title III, §304; Heartland Act, P.L. 110-343, Div. C, Title VII, Subtitle A, §702(e)(3).

[73] Job Creation Act, P.L. 107-147, Title III, §301(a) (codified at 26 U.S.C. §1400L(c)).

the earned income tax credit instead of the income from the year of the disaster.[74] This may have benefited taxpayers whose income was reduced in the year of the disaster. In general, taxpayers qualified only if the disaster caused them to be displaced from their principal place of abode.

Treasury Authority to Make Adjustments Relating to Status

KETRA, the GO Zone Act, and the Heartland Act all contained similar provisions that authorized the Treasury Secretary to make adjustments in the application of the tax laws for the tax years of the disaster and the immediate subsequent year so that temporary relocations due to the disaster did not cause taxpayers to lose any deduction or credit or to experience a change of filing status.[75]

Education Credits

Individuals with eligible tuition and related expenses may claim the Hope Scholarship or Lifetime Learning credit.[76] Under the law existing when KETRA, the GO Zone Act, and the Heartland Act were enacted, the Hope credit was 100% of the first $1,000 of eligible expenses plus 50% of the next $1,000 of eligible expenses, both adjusted for inflation. The maximum Lifetime Learning credit is and was 20% of up to $10,000 of eligible expenses. Beginning in 2009, the partially refundable American Opportunity Tax Credit (AOTC)[77] temporarily increased the Hope credit, allowing 100% of eligible expenses up to $2,000 plus 25% of the next $2,000 of eligible expenses.[78] Currently, 2012 is the last year in which taxpayers can claim the AOTC.

For individuals attending school in the GO Zone for 2005 and 2006, the GO Zone Act allowed certain non-tuition expenses (e.g., books, equipment, and room and board) to qualify for the Hope and Lifetime Learning credits; doubled the $1,000 limitations in the Hope credit to $2,000; and increased the 20% limitation in the Lifetime Learning credit to 40%.[79] The Heartland Act provided similar rules for students attending school in a Midwestern disaster area during 2008 or 2009.[80] However, to take advantage of this provision for 2009, taxpayers were required to waive application of the AOTC provisions.[81]

---

[74] KETRA, P.L. 109-73, Title IV, §406; GO Zone Act, P.L. 109-135, Title II, §201(a) (codified at 26 U.S.C. §1400S(d)); P.L. 110-343, Div. C, Title VII, Subtitle A, §702(d). The credits are found in IRC §§24 and 32. For discussion of them, see CRS Report R41873, *The Child Tax Credit: Current Law and Legislative History*, by Margot L. Crandall-Hollick; CRS Report RL31768, *The Earned Income Tax Credit (EITC): An Overview*, by Christine Scott.

[75] KETRA, P.L. 109-73, Title IV, §407; GO Zone Act, P.L. 109-135, §201(a) (codified at 26 U.S.C. §1400S(e)).

[76] 26 U.S.C. §25A. For information, see CRS Report R41967, *Higher Education Tax Benefits: Brief Overview and Budgetary Effects*, by Margot L. Crandall-Hollick.

[77] For information on the AOTC, see CRS Report R42561, *The American Opportunity Tax Credit: Overview, Analysis, and Policy Options*, by Margot L. Crandall-Hollick.

[78] 26 U.S.C. §25A(i)(1).

[79] GO Zone Act, P.L. 109-135, Title I, §102 (codified at 26 U.S.C. §1400O).

[80] Heartland Act, P.L. 110-343, Div. C, Title VII, Subtitle A, §702(d)(8).

[81] 26 U.S.C. §25A(i)(7).

Low-Income Housing Tax Credit

The low-income housing tax credit allows owners of qualified residential rental property to claim a credit over a 10-year period that is based on the costs of constructing, rehabilitating, or acquiring the building attributable to low-income units.[82] Owners may claim a credit based on 130% of the project's costs if the housing is in a low-income or difficult development area. Owners must be allocated the credit by a state. Each state is limited in the amount of credits it may allocate to the greater of $2,000,000 or $1.75 times the state's population (both are adjusted for inflation and are $2,525,000 and $2.20 for 2012),[83] with adjustments.

The GO Zone Act temporarily increased the credits available to Alabama, Louisiana, and Mississippi for use in the GO Zone by up to $18.00 multiplied by the state's population that was located in the GO Zone prior to the date of Hurricane Katrina.[84] It also temporarily treated the disaster zones as difficult development areas and used an alternate test for determining whether certain GO Zone projects qualified as low-income housing.[85] The Heartland Act permitted affected states to allocate additional amounts for use in the disaster area of up to $8.00 multiplied by the state's disaster area population.[86]

Rehabilitation Credit

Taxpayers may claim a credit equal to 10% of the qualifying expenditures to rehabilitate a qualified building or 20% of such expenditures for a certified historic structure.[87]

Both the GO Zone Act and the Heartland Act temporarily increased these percentages to 13% and 26% for rehabilitating qualifying buildings and structures damaged by the applicable disasters.[88]

New Markets Tax Credit

Under the new markets tax credit, taxpayers are allocated a credit for investments made in qualified community development entities.[89] The credit is claimed over a period of seven years and equals the amount of the investment multiplied by a percentage: 5% for the first three years and 6% for the next four years. The credit was capped at $2 billion for 2005 and $3.5 billion for 2006 and 2007. The most recent year for which it was allocated was 2011, when it was capped at $3.5 million. There is no allocation for 2012.

---

[82] 26 U.S.C. §42. For more information, see CRS Report RL33904, *The Low-Income Housing Tax Credit: A Framework for Evaluation*, by Pamela J. Jackson.

[83] Rev. Proc. 2011-52, 2011-2 C.B. 701. For 2013, the amounts will be increased to $2,590,000 and $2.25. Rev. Proc. 2012-41, 2012 IRB LEXIS 505 (Oct. 18, 2012).

[84] It also increased the credits available to Florida and Texas in 2006 by $3,500,000 for each state.

[85] GO Zone Act, P.L. 109-135, Title I, §101(a) (codified at 26 U.S.C. §1400N(c)).

[86] Heartland Act, P.L. 110-343, Div. C, Title VII, Subtitle A, §702(d)(2). The act also provided an additional allocation for Texas and Louisiana, which had been affected by Hurricane Act, equal to $16.00 multiplied by the state's population located in the specified counties.

[87] 26 U.S.C. §47.

[88] GO Zone Act, P.L. 109-135, Title I, §101(a) (codified at 26 U.S.C. §1400N(h)); Heartland Act, P.L. 110-343, Div. C, Title VII, Subtitle A, §702(a)(1).

[89] 26 U.S.C. §45D.

The GO Zone Act increased the cap by $300 million for 2005 and 2006 and by $400 million for 2007, and it allocated these amounts to entities making low-income community investments in the GO Zone.[90]

Small Timber Producers

Under IRC Section 194, taxpayers may expense up to $10,000 of qualifying reforestation expenditures. Under IRC Section 172, the general rule is that taxpayers may carry net operating losses back for two years.

The GO Zone Act created two special rules for timber producers with less than 501 acres of timber property: it (1) increased the Section 194 limit by up to $10,000 for expenditures made for qualified timber property in the applicable disaster zones; and (2) increased the Section 172 carry back period to five years for certain losses attributable to timber property in those zones.[91]

Public Utility Losses

Under IRC Section 172, certain net operating losses, called specified liability losses, may be carried back for 10 years. Under IRC Section 165(i), certain disaster losses may be deducted in the year prior to the disaster.

The GO Zone Act treated public utility casualty losses as a Section 172 loss and allowed GO Zone public utility disaster losses to be deducted in the fifth taxable year preceding the disaster.[92]

---

[90] GO Zone Act, P.L. 109-135, Title I, §101(a) (codified at 26 U.S.C. §1400N(m)).

[91] GO Zone Act, P.L. 109-135, Title I, §101(a) (codified at 26 U.S.C. §1400N(i)).

[92] GO Zone Act, P.L. 109-135, Title I, §101(a) (codified at 26 U.S.C. §1400N(j)).

Appendix. Comparison Among Laws

Table A-1. Comparison of Temporary Provisions Contained in Prior Acts

(Note the provisions are not necessarily identical; see discussion in report)

Provision (links to relevant part in report)	Job Creation and Worker Assistance Act of 2002 — Terrorist attacks of 9/11/2011	Katrina Emergency Tax Relief Act of 2005 — Hurricane Katrina	GO Zone Act of 2005 — Hurricanes Katrina, Rita, and Wilma	Heartland Disaster Tax Relief Act of 2008 and other provisions in P.L. 110-343 — 2007 Midwest storms	Heartland Disaster Tax Relief Act of 2008 and other provisions in P.L. 110-343 — Disasters between 2007-2009
Casualty Losses		Yes	Yes	Yes	Yes
Expensing	Yes		Yes	Yes	Yes
Net Operating Losses			Yes	Yes	Yes
Bonus Depreciation	Yes		Yes		Yes
Mortgage Revenue Bonds		Yes	Yes		Yes
Expensing of Environmental Remediation Costs			Yesª		Yes (but not limited to those disasters)ª
Charitable Contributions of Inventory		Yes (but not limited to disasters)ᵇ			Yes (but not limited to disasters)ᵇ
Involuntary Conversions		Yes	Yes	Yes	
Discharge of Indebtedness		Yes		Yes	
Retirement Plan Distributions		Yes	Yes	Yes	
Work Opportunity Tax Credit	Yes	Yes			
Retention Credit		Yes	Yes	Yes	
Employer-Provided Housing			Yes	Yes	
Tax-Exempt Bonds	Yes		Yes	Yes	
Tax Credit Bonds			Yes	Yes	
Gulf Coast Recovery Bonds			Yes		
Limits on Charitable Deductions		Yes	Yes	Yes	
Housing Exemption		Yes		Yes	
Mileage Rate and Reimbursement		Yes		Yes	

Provision (links to relevant part in report)	Job Creation and Worker Assistance Act of 2002 Terrorist attacks of 9/11/2011	Katrina Emergency Tax Relief Act of 2005 Hurricane Katrina	GO Zone Act of 2005 Hurricanes Katrina, Rita, and Wilma	Heartland Disaster Tax Relief Act of 2008 and other provisions in P.L. 110-343	
				2007 Midwest storms	Disasters between 2007-2009
Leasehold Improvements	Yes				
Credit Computations		Yes	Yes	Yes	
Treasury Authority to Make Adjustments Relating to Status		Yes	Yes	Yes	
Education Credits			Yes	Yes	
Low-Income Housing Tax Credit			Yes	Yes	
Rehabilitation Credit			Yes	Yes	
New Markets Tax Credit			Yes		
Small Timber Producers			Yes		
Public Utility Losses			Yes		

Source: Congressional Research Service

Notes:

a. The remediation expensing provision (IRC Section 198) is not limited to federally declared disasters or specific disasters. It was temporary when enacted and was extended several times, but has now expired. The Heartland Act was among those laws that extended Section198. Heartland Act, P.L. 110-343, Div. C, Title III, §318. The GO Zone Act had also extended it, but only for those costs for contaminated sites in the GO Zone, as well as treating petroleum products as a hazardous substance. GO Zone Act, P.L. 109-135, Title I, §101(a) (codified at 26 U.S.C. §1400N(g)).

b. KETRA provided special rules regarding donations of food and book inventory, neither of which was limited to donations related to the hurricane, but both of which were originally set to expire on December 31, 2005. The provisions have been extended several times since then, including by the Heartland Act (as part of its tax extenders package, rather than its disaster relief provisions). Heartland Act, P.L. 110-343, Div. C, Title III, §§323, 324. Most recently, both provisions were extended through December 31, 2011. P.L. 111-312 ("Tax Relief, Unemployment Insurance Reauthorization, and Job Creation Act of 2010"), Subtitle C, §§740(a), 741(a).

Author Contact Information

Erika K. Lunder
Legislative Attorney
elunder@crs.loc.gov, 7-4538

Carol A. Pettit
Legislative Attorney
cpettit@crs.loc.gov, 7-9496

Jennifer Teefy
Information Research Specialist
jteefy@crs.loc.gov, 7-7625